Whitework

Women Stitching Identity

Laurel M. Horton
with Dr. Kate Brown
& Dr. Margaret Ordoñez

*The Kentucky Museum at Western Kentucky University
and Kentucky Historical Society*

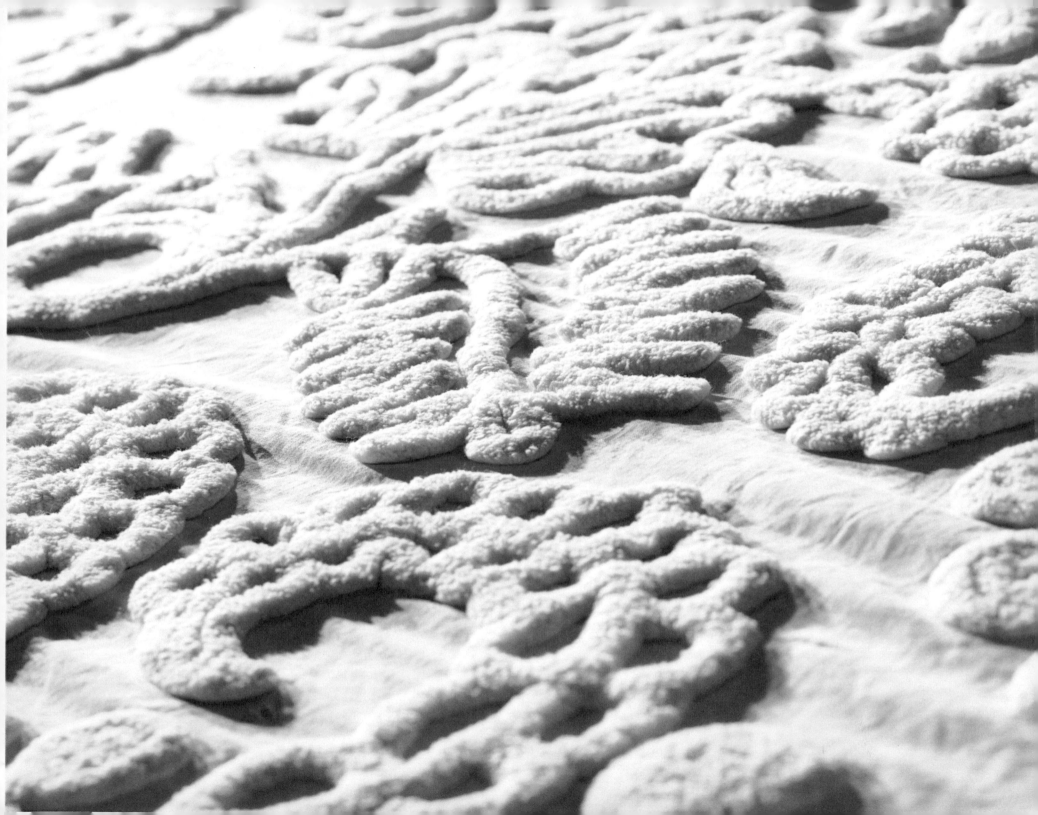

Contents

Preface

European Influences

Early Republic Era

Why White?

White Women

Enslaved Makers

The Strange Family

Legacies

Creation

Conservation

Quilts & Counterpanes of Kentucky Women

About the Guest Curator and Contributors

Sponsors

Donors of the Textiles

Sources

Laurel M. Horton views Rebecca Smith Washington's whitework quilt during collection photography, March 2021. Photo by Clinton Lewis/WKU.

Preface

American textile scholarship matured in the fourth quarter of the 20th century, as academic and independent researchers examined quilts and woven coverlets within larger cultural contexts. However, individual scholars generally work within a single textile genre, each with its specialized publications and networks. Within each of the individual textile genres, quilted, embroidered and woven white bedcovers occupy the margins. One must look at the area where these peripheries overlap to see that, taken together, embellished white bedcovers form a body of work in themselves. Then it becomes possible to overlook the borders between techniques and recognize the intrinsic commonality.

In 2006, I realized that no one had done substantive research on "old white bedcovers," and I decided to address that lack. Having focused on patchwork traditions for thirty years, I knew that this new project would include not just whole-cloth quilts, but also embroidered and woven counterpanes. After looking at hundreds of examples in museum and private collections, I needed to define a more manageable geographic area. As it turned out, my home state of Kentucky offered the ideal laboratory for this study.

Made during a time when women had no public voice, white quilts and counterpanes – called "whitework" – survive as material records of both personal identity and collective political expression. American women who made whitework between 1790 and 1830 were providing utilitarian textiles for their beds, as well as expressing personal preferences through the motifs found on the textiles. Yet their meaning was much deeper: the women were expressing support of patriotic efforts to reduce dependence on imported British textiles, emphasizing their new identity of American independence while maintaining a cultural tradition that began in the early Medieval period.

These textiles also counteract traditional narratives of Early Republic women, especially along the frontier regions like Kentucky. Historically, women's lives, activities, and creative expressions have been undervalued, even trivialized. While a number of authors published books about quilts in the first half of the 20th century, their perspectives were heavily influenced by Colonial Revival notions of an America created by self-sufficient pioneer ancestors. These elegant white bedcovers simply did not fit into a narrative of resourceful frontier women making patchwork quilts to keep their families warm in their drafty cabins.

Further examination of these textiles also reveals a narrative not largely addressed in Colonial Revival notions: evidence of the participation of enslaved Blacks in the creation of whitework textiles. These stories add critical context while rectifying an oversight in histories of the Early Republic frontier.

This exhibition honors the individual makers and their descendants, but it also offers, for the first time, an opportunity to understand these textiles as documents of women's collective political expression and the conflicting values of American independence. The collections of the Kentucky Historical Society and the Kentucky Museum house ample documented examples to illustrate all the themes that emerged from my research. I am grateful that these two fine museums have partnered to make this exhibition possible.

Laurel Horton
Guest Curator

Quilted bedcover with scenes from the legend of Tristan, Sicily, about 1400, one of the earliest extant white quilted bedcovers. © Victoria & Albert Museum, London.

The Exhibition

Handwoven counterpane produced in Bolton, Lancashire, England, from American-grown cotton, between 1790 and 1820. Kentucky Museum, 2857.

European Influences

Fine white quilted bedcovers were associated with royal families in Europe during the 1300s, and the tradition was emulated by courtiers and other wealthy families. By the mid-1600s, a cottage industry in Provence employed about 2,000 needleworkers to hand-quilt bedcovers and other textiles for export to consumers throughout the world. During the industrial revolution of the late 1700s, elaborate hand-operated mechanical looms could produce products that imitated hand-quilted textiles. Soon British mills, particularly those in Manchester, were producing large numbers of woven "quilts" in a wide variety of designs.

A second method for weaving whitework arose in Bolton, Lancashire in the 1700s. Local weavers were familiar with a simple weft-loop technique, which involved manually pulling selected weft yarns into raised tufts to create designs. By the 1750s, Bolton weavers refined the process to create intricate floral and pictorial patterns on double-wide looms, producing counterpanes without center seams.

The whitework textiles made by American women between 1790 and 1820 were influenced by these fashionable woven bedcovers imported from England.

"Kentucky Landscape – 1832" by James Pierce Barton depicts the agrarian paradise promoted to Kentucky settlers. Cincinnati Museum Center at Union Terminal, CHS.1913.1.

Early Republic Era

During the early republic period—roughly 1776 to 1820—the American nation won her independence (and maintained it during the War of 1812), created a constitutional republic, and began navigating the challenges of federalism. This period also marked the beginning of a long transformation in the American economy—what historian Charles Sellers deemed the "market revolution"—into modernity.

Economic change encompassed: the diversification of the American economy toward manufacturing; the construction of turnpikes and canals; the increased interconnectedness of American farmers, new manufacturers, commercial hubs, and distant world markets; the rise of the insurance industry underwriting the risks involved in trade; the transformation in the law of property, contracts, and torts also underwriting those risks; the facilitation of economic development by a national government with newly ratified constitutional powers; and all of this eventually ushering in an age of industrialization.

In addition to the sheer breadth and scope of economic change during this period, the transformation was even more astounding for the fact that the new American nation was born mired in crushing war debt, inflation, economic recession, the impotence of its confederation government, and the ever-present uncertainty of the republic's fate.

Given this starting point, the accomplishments of the Philadelphia Constitutional Convention, George Washington's administration, and in particular, secretary of the treasury Alexander Hamilton's brilliant funding, assumption, banking, and manufacturing development plans seem even more incredible for what they achieved: righting a sinking economic ship and successfully steering it toward growth and prosperity. Even with bumps along the way—cyclical recessions and Thomas Jefferson's embargo, for example—the American economic transformation raced full steam ahead.

Opposite, top: "View of South Street, from Maiden Lane, New York City" by Willliam James Bennett, ca. 1827, held by the Metropolitan Museum of Art, The Edward W. C. Arnold Collection of New York Prints, Maps, and Pictures, Bequest of Edward W. C. Arnold, 1954.

Opposite, circle left: Mother and Child in White, c. 1790, by unknown artist, held by National Gallery of Art, Gift of Edgar William and Bernice Chrysler Garbisch .

Opposite, circle right: "Portrait of a Young Woman" by Mather Brown, 1801, Metropolitan Museum of Art, Gift of Caroline Newhouse, 1965.

This page, at right: Openwork fruit basket, ca. 1770–72, manufactured by the American China Manufactory, the second earliest porcelain manufacturer in the United States. Metropolitan Museum of Art, 2018.407, Purchase, Ronald S. Kane Bequest and Anthony W. and Lulu C. Wang and Robert L. Froelich Gifts, 2018.

Plate VI.

W. Hincks Del. & Sculp.

To the RIGHT HON.^{BLE} the EARL of MOIRA,
THIS Plate, TAKEN ON THE SPOT IN THE COUNTY OF DOWNE,
Representing Spinning, Reeling with the Clock Reel, and Boiling the Yarn;
Is most respectfully Dedicated by his Lordships

1. Spinning
2. Reeling
3. Boiling the

All Americans were touched by this economic growth and all participated in it, including those whom the historical record tends to obscure. Women were just as crucial to economic transformation as they were for raising the next generation of civically engaged, republican citizens. Women participated in household economies, producing and selling surplus crops or home-manufactures.

They also engaged in politics, voting where possible (New Jersey granted qualified women the right to vote from 1776 until 1807) but still speaking their minds about politics where not. Yet, even when women did not possess the political rights enjoyed by an increasingly broad swath of (white) men, they whole-heartedly engaged with economic politics throughout the early republic and into the Age of Jackson.

Dr. Kate Brown

Opposite page: "To the right hon'able the Earl of Moira, this plate, taken on the spot in the County of Downe, representing spinning, reeling with the clock reel, and boiling the yarn" by William Hincks, London : Publish'd as the Act directs, by R. Pollard, Spafields, 1791 June 20. Photography courtesy Library of Congress. This page, above: Close-up of Embroidered Sampler by Elizabeth Easton, 1795. Made in Newport, Rhode Island, United States, this sampler was part of Elizabeth's education in learning the techniques required in more complex embroidery. Metropolitan Museum of Art, Rogers Fund, 1913.

Why White?

White household objects have had a long association with gentility and refinement in European society. American scholars have further documented a "whitening of America" beginning in the late 1700s, as consumers expressed a preference for white dishes, building materials, clothing, and household textiles. The onset of this trend coincided with the period of the American Revolution, with which it became entwined.

Patriots encouraged efforts to increase home production of textiles as a moral imperative to purify themselves from the polluting influence of dependence on British goods. Patriotic women and girls wore dresses of undyed home-produced linen instead of colorful printed calico and chintz fabrics from British factories. Even women from wealthy families made their own white embellished bedcovers instead of purchasing fancy woven counterpanes and quilts.

"Portrait of the John Speed Smith Family," 1819, by Chester Harding (1792-1866). Collection of the Speed Art Museum, Louisville, Kentucky, 1956.14. Gift of William Stucky.

However, during the antebellum period, the movement toward whiteness emphasized and intensified the disparity marked by race. The clothing worn by enslaved people was typically dyed blue or brown. White and Black people may have lived and worked in proximity, but the colors they wore served as a constant reminder of the difference in status.

Awareness of these racial implications expands our understanding of the work of enslaved artisans in fiber and cloth production for white bedcovers. Enslaved spinners and weavers would have noted the incongruity of working white fabric with their skilled hands.

Above: "The Old Plantation" attributed to John Rose, c. 1785-1795, depicts slaves dancing on a South Carolina plantation wearing clothing of their own manufacture. The colors are typical of "slave cloth." Abby Aldrich Rockefeller Folk Art Museum, Williamsburg, Virginia.

White Women

At the heart of this exhibition are young Kentucky women who made white quilts and counterpanes between 1790 and 1820. Although they were not acquainted with one another, they were among the participants in a collective expression of patriotism.

They had much in common. They were born between 1772 and 1802, either in Virginia or in Kentucky to parents who emigrated from Virginia to Kentucky. Their fathers had served in the Revolutionary War while their mothers had engaged in domestic textile manufacture as a patriotic cause, and they passed those skills and motivations to their daughters. Historian Mary Beth Norton found that "women's experience of the struggle gave them a newfound confidence of themselves. The line between male and female behavior became less well defined." According to historian Linda K. Kerber:

> *"Instead, women were left to form their own political character. They devised their own interpretation of what the Revolution had meant to them as women, and they began to invent an ideology of citizenship that merged the domestic domain of the preindustrial woman with the new public ideology of individual responsibility and civic virtue."*

These literal daughters of the American Revolution created white quilts and counterpanes to document their identity as women in the New Republic and in the "New Eden" of Kentucky, which Thomas Jefferson imagined as an agrarian paradise. These heirloom textiles were valued by the makers' descendants, who passed them down along with oral narratives that identified the makers and emphasized the maker's involvement in textile production.

At left: "Study for Labor" by Kenyon Cox, ca. 1870. Smithsonian American Art Museum, Bequest of Allyn Cox, 1983.31.5.

Public Sale.

Will be sold to the highest bidder for cash in hand, on

Tuesday the 14th day of June,

At Robard's & Curd's Store, about 3 miles from the mouth of Dick's river, Mercer county, Six or Eight likely *NEGROES*, to satisfy a decree or judgment of the Jessamine circuit court.

BEN. BRADSHAW,

Exe'r. of B. BRADSHAW, Dec'd. and Agent for Curd's Heirs.

June 6th 1836.

Enslaved Makers

Among those who settled Kentucky were enslaved Americans of African descent (Blacks). Undocumented field hands prepared the fields, planted seeds, and tended the crops. Skilled spinners converted the fibers into various types of threads and yarns. Highly trained, weavers needed to know the loom set-up for each type of fabric required, which might range from plain sheeting to pattern-woven textures.

The family narratives accompanying whitework often include a statement that the attributed maker spun the yarn and wove the cloth. In some cases, particularly makers whose households did not include enslaved workers, these statements are believable. But slaveholders often claimed the results of enslaved labor as their own, in such statements as, "I grew a fine crop of cotton this year." While some women did their own spinning and weaving, others relegated the work to enslaved artisans. Fiber analysis confirms that most of the yarns and threads in these textiles were spun by hand, but we don't know by whose hands.

Dr. Mrs. Apphia Rouzee   Cr.

In a/c with Jesse Taylor

1806				
To weaveing 1 piece Cloth	30 yds	@ 4	0 – 10 – 0
„ Ditto	31	do	0 – 10 – 4
„ Ditto	50	do	0 – 16 – 8
„ Ditto	24	do	0 – 8 – 0
„ Ditto	42	do	0 – 14 – 0
1 Blanket furnished your Girl		13/6	0 – 13 – 6

£ 3 – 12 – 6

1807				
To Weaving 1 piece Cloth	41 yds	@ 4	0 – 13 – 8
„ Ditto 1 do	31	do	0 – 10 – 4

£ 4 – 16 – 6

Cr.

1805.	By hire of your Girl Philice	£1 – 8 – 0	
1806	„ ditto — do for this year	3 – –	4 – 8 – 0

E.E.

Balance due J. Taylor   0 – 8 – 6

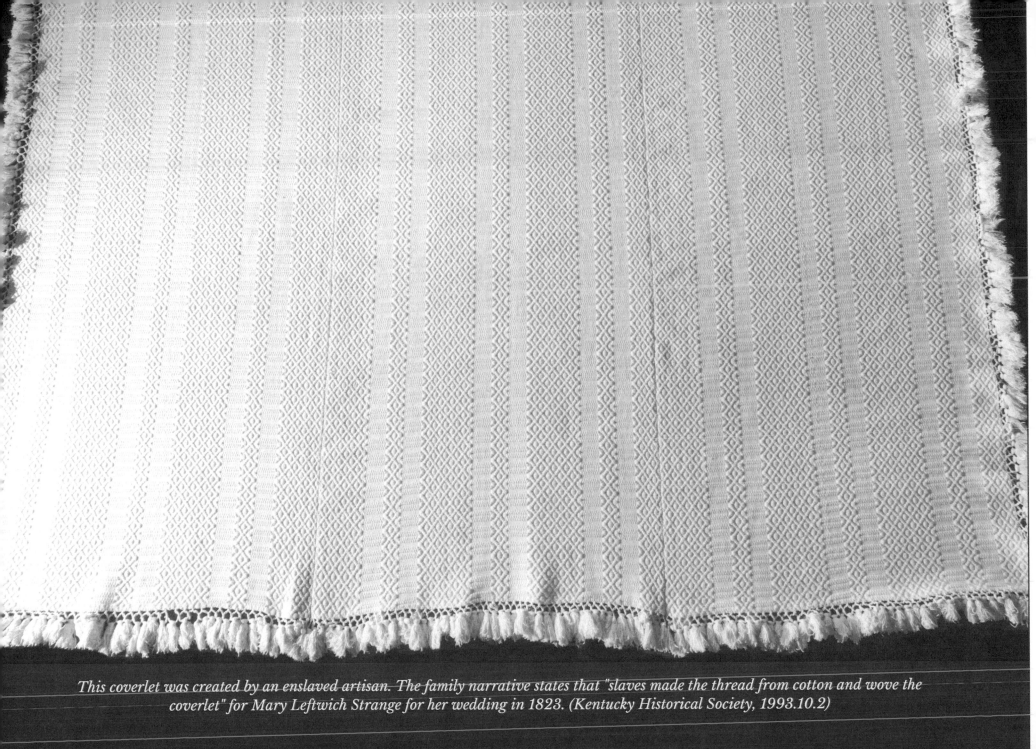

This coverlet was created by an enslaved artisan. The family narrative states that "slaves made the thread from cotton and wove the coverlet" for Mary Leftwich Strange for her wedding in 1823. (Kentucky Historical Society, 1993.10.2)

Post Office *Bowling Green*

Dwelling-houses numbered in the order of visitation.	Families numbered in the order of visitation.	The name of every person whose usual place of abode on the first day of June, 1860, was in this family.	Age.	Sex.	Color, White, black, or mulatto.	Profession, Occupation, or Trade of each person, male and female, over 15 years of age.	Value of Real Estate.	Value of Personal Estate.	Place of Birth, Naming the State, Territory, or Country.	Married within the year.	Attended School within the year.	Persons over 20 y'rs of age who cannot read & write.	Whether deaf and dumb, blind, insane, idiotic, pauper, or convict.	
38	1117	1117	Gideon McDaniel	60	"		Farmer	10125	26540	Tenn	✓			38
39		Mary	57	F					Virs	✓			39
40		Subell	18	"		Farm hand			Ky		✓		40

U.S. Census pages, dated 1860 (top) and 1870 (bottom), detailing the property value for the McDaniel family before and after the Civil War. In 1860, their personal estate was $26,540; after the war, in 1870, it fell to $4,800.

Page No. 22 }

☞ Inquiries numbered 7, 16, and 17 are not to be asked in respect to infants. Inquiries numbered 11, 12, 15, 16, 17, 19, and 20 are to be answered (if at all) merely by an affirmative mark, as /.

SCHEDULE 1.—Inhabitants in *Elk Spring District*, in the County of *Warren*, State of *Kentucky*, enumerated by me on the 23 day of *Sept*, 1870.

Post Office: *Smiths Grove Ky*   *E. F. Kinnaird*, Ass't Marshal.

		The name of every person whose place of abode on the first day of June, 1870, was in this family.	Age at last birthday. If under 1 year, give months in fractions, thus, 1/12	Sex.—Male (M.), Female (F.)	Color—White (W.), Black (B.), Mulatto (M.), Chinese (C.), Indian (I.)	Profession, Occupation, or Trade of each person, male or female.	Value of Real Estate.	Value of Personal Estate.	Place of Birth, naming State or Territory of U. S.; or the Country, if of foreign birth.	Father of foreign birth.	Mother of foreign birth.	If born within the year, state month (Jan., Feb., &c.)	If married within the year, state month (Jan., Feb., &c.)	Attended school within the year.	Cannot read.	Cannot write.	Whether deaf and dumb, blind, insane, or idiotic.	Male Citizen of U.S. of 21 years of age and upwards.	Male Citizen of U.S. of 21 years and upwards whose right to vote is denied or abridged on other grounds than rebellion or other crime.	
			4	5	6	7	8	9	10	11	12	13	14	15	16	17	18	19	20	
		Eva	12	F	W	At School			So											18
19	149 157	McDaniel Subell E	28	M	W	Farmer	4500		So										✓	19
20		Sarah Bell	22	F	W	Keeping House			So											20
21		Mary L	1	F	W				So											21
22		Gideon	63	M	W	Farmer	4800	5840	Virginia										✓	22
23		Mary L	66	F	W	Keeping House			So											23
24			19	M	W				Kentucky											24

The Strange Family

Census records and family oral histories help identify potential links of counterpanes to enslaved workers. Descendants of Mary Strange McDaniel noted that "slaves made the thread from cotton and wove the coverlet" for Mary's wedding. According to the 1820 Census, Mary's mother owned 19 enslaved workers, including three women.

In 1823, Mary married Rev. Gideon McDaniel and they relocated to Warren County, Kentucky. In 1840, their household listed 20 enslaved people. In the following decades, the number of the enslaved changed slightly, reflecting a few more births than deaths.

By 1860, just before the outbreak of the Civil War, the McDaniels' personal estate included 24 enslaved workers and was valued at $26,540. In 1870, the effects of war and emancipation are reflected in valuation of their personal property at $4,800, one fifth of the pre-war amount. These figures show the degree to which the wealth of antebellum farmers was built upon the backs of enslaved Blacks.

"Homespun" by Thomas Eakins, 1881. Metropolitan Museum of Art, courtesy Fletcher Fund, 1925.

Legacies

Revolutionary War veterans received land grants in Kentucky in lieu of payment for their service. These grants disregarded established treaties between the British and Indigenous tribes. To whites, Kentucky offered fertile land and expanded opportunities as a "New Eden," which Thomas Jefferson imagined as an agrarian paradise. Veterans' wives and daughters found themselves on the threshold of a new life, where their skills would contribute to an imagined future of peace and plenty. In reality, settlers forcibly removed Indigenous peoples from their ancestral lands. Settlers were also sometimes supported by enslaved Blacks, whose unpaid labor made considerable contributions to individual households and the emerging economy.

Though the rhetoric of American independence promised equality, the framers of the new government only extended full citizenship to property-owning white men – excluding some men and all women and people of color. These decisions profoundly impacted America up to the present day. Though the names of countless Indigenous and enslaved individuals remain unknown, their legacy of suffering persists in the ongoing socioeconomic inequalities and race-based violence experienced by people of color today.

Creation and Conservation

Creation

The climate of Kentucky, like that of Virginia, was conducive to the large-scale cultivation of flax, the plant whose fiber is spun into yarn then woven into linen cloth. Flax production was labor intensive, and processing a crop took over a year from planting to finished fiber. The harvested plants were allowed to rot, then threshed to remove seeds and woody parts. The resulting fibers were beaten with a swingling-knife (a wooden paddle), then drawn through a hatchel, or hackle, to separate the long flax fibers from the shorter straw-like tow. The flax fibers were spun into fine thread, and tow was used to make bagging, twine, rope, and clothing for enslaved persons.

The harvesting of cotton was also labor intensive, but the introduction of the cotton gin in the 1790s drastically reduced the time and labor needed to separate the seeds tightly embedded in the cotton fibers. The cleaned fibers were then carded to prepare for spinning. Although Kentucky's short growing season and transportation difficulties limited large-scale commercial cotton production, many families planted cotton for their own use and local markets. As revealed by fiber analysis, spinners typically blended the short fibers of cotton with longer, stronger flax fibers as they spun their thread.

Quilters enhanced the three-dimensional effect of their work by inserting close rows of a thicker yarn to create raised motifs. Close "stipple" quilting in the background provides additional contrast. (Kentucky Museum, 1806)

A skilled embroiderer worked multiple stitches in motifs designed by a professional designer and stamped on fabric for a purchased kit. (Kentucky Museum, 1993.14.1)

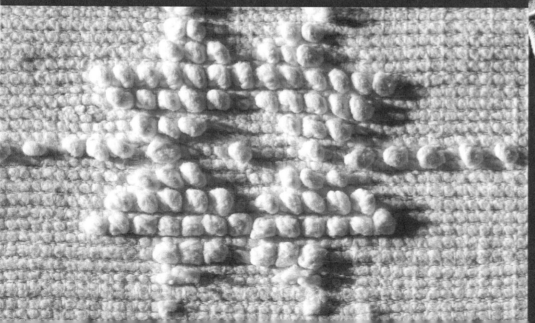

An unknown British weaver inserted thicker weft yarns at regular intervals to create ribs and used a small hook to pull certain yarns into loops to create a design of raised motifs in this Bolton counterpane. (Kentucky Museum, 2857)

Whitework designs are produced by manipulating white thread or yarn on a foundation fabric to form raised patterns and figures for a three-dimensional effect. Three primary techniques were used by the makers featured in this exhibition.

Quilting involves stitching through a textile "sandwich" consisting of two fabric sheets with a fluffy layer of batting between. **Corded quilting** results from inserting a thick yarn through channels formed by two parallel lines of stitching. A corded quilt may also contain a layer of batting or a backing.

Below from left: Examples of quilting (Kentucky Museum, 2652) and corded quilting (Kentucky Historical Society, 1980.12.2).

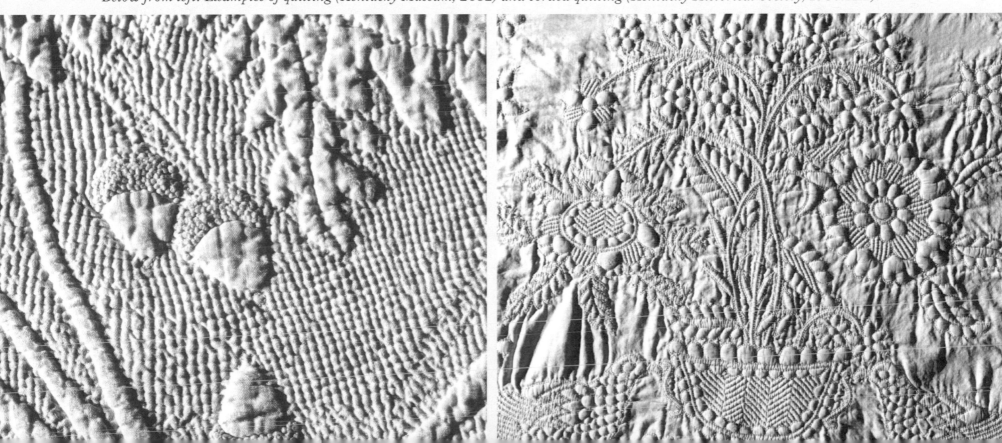

Surface embroidery offers a large vocabulary of stitches to form designs close to the foundation fabric. Various stitches can be combined to form floral, geometric, or figural motifs. **Open work** describes techniques that create perforations though the ground fabric, such as eyelets, drawn or pulled work removing or deflecting threads, and Dresden work, which emulates the airy complexity of lace. **Raised embroidery** uses a thick yarn to produce knots, loops, and/or tufts to intensify the dimensional effect of motifs. This form of embroidery was later described as candlewick, a misnomer.

Below from left: Examples of open work (Kentucky Historical Society, 1981.11), tufting (Kentucky Historical Society, 1981.17), and raised embroidery (Kentucky Historical Society, 1981.19).

Plain weaving produced the foundation fabrics for white quilts and embroidered counterpanes. The warp yarns are stretched tightly from the back of the loom through the heddles to the front, and the weft yarns are inserted across the loom by the weaver. **Patterned weaving** describes the many ways that weavers could create more complex designs by making adjustments to different parts of the loom. **Weft-loop weaving** involves the periodic insertion of a secondary thick weft yarn into an otherwise plain weave structure. These larger yarns form horizontal ribs across the surface, and they can be selectively pulled into loops to form a simple pattern or complex figural motifs.

Below from left: Examples of patterned weaving (Kentucky Historical Society, 1993.10.2)
and weft-loop weaving (Kentucky Museum, 2020.2.1).

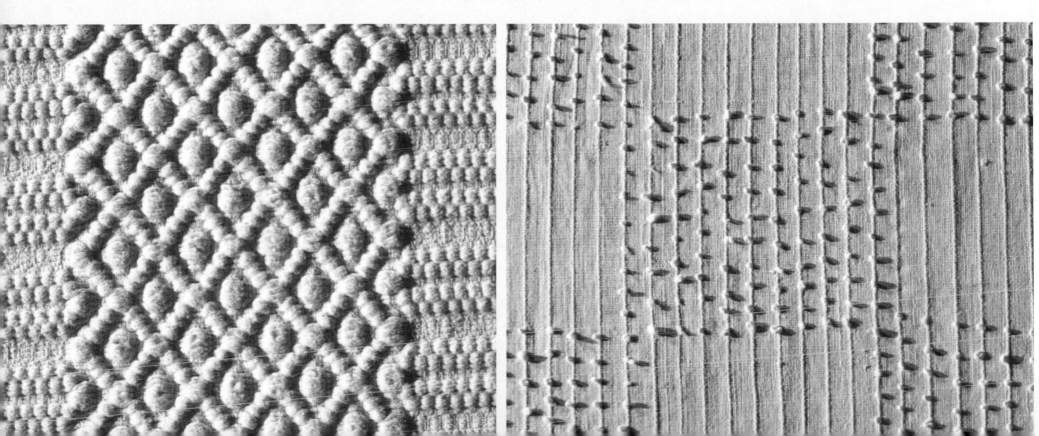

Ultrviolet light (dark field) analysis of textiles reveals their composition. Above, flax fibers are identifiable by stiff, straight appearance and cross markings. Below, a blend of cotton and flax is identified through the lack of cellulose (lower left fiber, indicating cotton) and two very narrow flax fibers (center).

Conservation

The first step in object conservation is analysis. Using different tools, textile conservators determine the fiber content as well as yarn and fabric construction. These guide their decisions in choosing treatments that will help stabilize the textiles for safe exhibition.

For whitework textiles, conservators look for whether the fibers are flax, cotton, or a flax-cotton blend. This involves dark field analysis – the use of ultraviolet light to look at fiber characteristics. Flax fibers are characterized by stiff, straight appearance and cross marking (often v-shaped), and a central canal (line running through the center). Flax fibers also vary in their diameters. Cotton fibers have convolutions— called "twists"—and a unique cross section that is bean shaped, producing two ridges along the sides of fibers. The frequency of twists varies.

Blends of cotton and flax are identified by the presence of both types of fibers. In the bottom picture at left, a wide, flat, immature cotton fiber on the far lower left does not have much cellulose deposited, resulting in a very thin fiber that seems to twist. An instant clue that flax is present are the two very narrow diameter fibers curving vertically in the center. Late-eighteenth and early-nineteenth century fabrics are often cataloged as being made of cotton, but microscopic examination reveals that many of them are blends of flax and cotton.

Fiber content affects appearance, air permeability, and wicking of moisture. This fabric in the Toomey counterpane (Kentucky Historical Society, 1981.11) has flax warp yarns (vertical) and fuzzy weft yarns (horizontal) made of a flax and cotton blend. The smoothness of the flax warp creates a reflective surface, and the addition of cotton increases permeability and wicking in the fabric.

The yarns in this Henry counterpane fabric (Kentucky Historical Society, 2000.21.1) are typical of most of the exhibition's fabrics: they are blends of cotton and flax and are single yarns spun in the Z direction (follow the direction of the line in the middle of the letter Z). They have varying diameters and amount of spin, possibly indicative of hand spinning.

The two-ply sewing thread in the Lafon counterpane (Kentucky Historical Society, 1935.2) is twisted in the Z direction (singles are s-spun). Its distinctive sheen is indicative of flax; the fabric yarns are a cotton/flax blend.

Most of the fabrics in the exhibition are plain weaves with a higher warp count than weft. The fabric count of the Helm counterpane (Kentucky Museum, 1987.86.1) is ~23 x 16–17 yarns per centimeter (scale in mm) indicating that the warp yarns are horizontal in the picture.

A few fabrics have weaving errors as in the Darrough counterpane (Kentucky Historical Society, 1937.7).

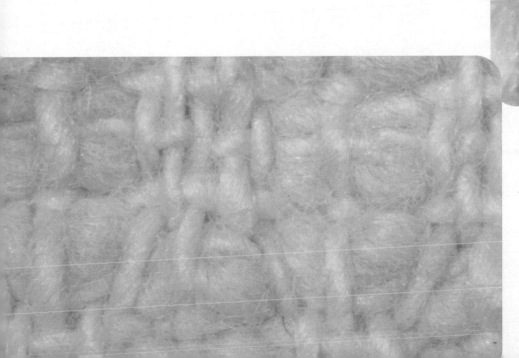

Most of the fabrics in the quilts and counterpanes are plain weaves, but this counterpane made by enslaved Black artisans (Kentucky Historical Society, 1993.10.2) has the design woven in. Using yarns of different diameters and amount of spin adds more variation to the pattern.

41

Repairs and Stabilization

Some of the textiles had tears, holes, and losses of fabric. Treatments aimed to stabilize the damage, preventing further tears or widening of holes. This treatment is about conservation (as opposed to restoration, which aims to make the textile look new). In making these repairs, conservators aim to use fabrics and threads whose colors and thread counts match the original fabric as closely as possible.

Washington quilt (Kentucky Museum, 2652) before (left) and after (right) treatment.

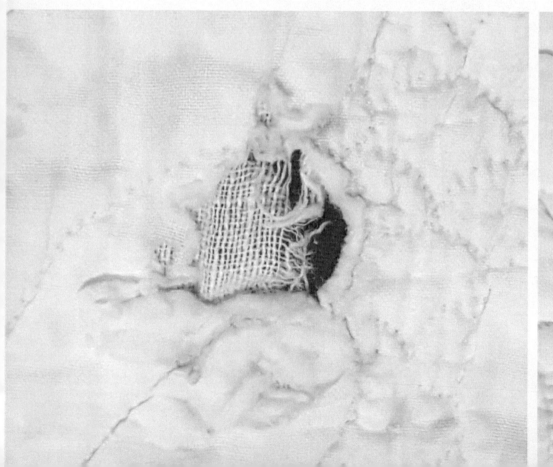

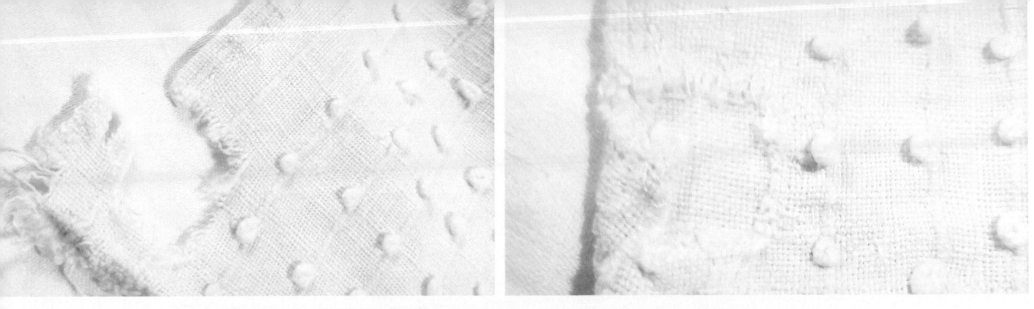

O'Neal counterpane (Kentucky Museum, 2021.2.1) before (left) and after (right) treatment

To repair holes and tears, an underlay of new fabric helps stabilize the original threads while replacing the loss of fabric. The repairs shown on this page were done by Kay Papenfuss, an intern from Austin Peay University.

Helm counterpane (Kentucky Museum, 1987.86.2) before (left) and after (right) treatment

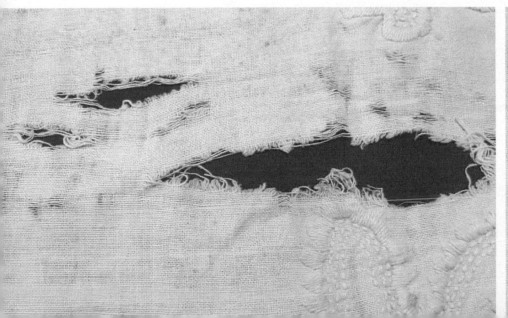

Previous Repairs

Some of the textiles had previously been repaired, by both skillful and less-practiced hands. Prior repairs that successfully stabilized damage without causing harm were not altered. But some of the repairs insufficiently supported the textile or were causing additional strain; these repairs were replaced. For example, the Bolton counterpane – shown below – had prior repairs that expanded the space between yarns. This lengthened the counterpane on that side and resulted in additional stress on the rest of the counterpane. The old repairs were removed and a new underlay repositioned the yarns, allowing the textile to hang straighter.

Bolton counterpane (Kentucky Museum. 2857) before (left) and after (right) treatment.

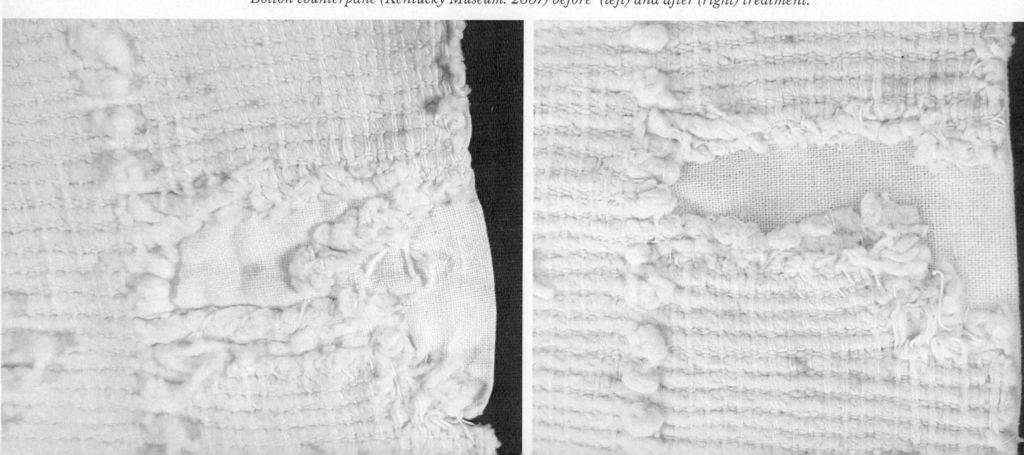

Wet-Cleaning

The next step in conservation is wet-cleaning the textiles. This helps rehydrate fibers, relax fold lines, and lessen discoloration, thus improving the textiles' appearance.

Discoloration results from use and storage of textiles. Stress from being slept under or draped across mattresses results in longer stains, while liquid spills or leaks during storage leave stains. Many of the textiles had been folded and stored in chests, trunks, or boxes that were acidic, thus degrading and staining the fabric.

Wren quilt (Kentucky Museum, 1806) has stain patterns that are the result of being slept under.

Marseilles quilt (Kentucky Museum, 1961.1.16) had evidence of liquid spills or leaks onto the fabric, resulting in smaller stains.

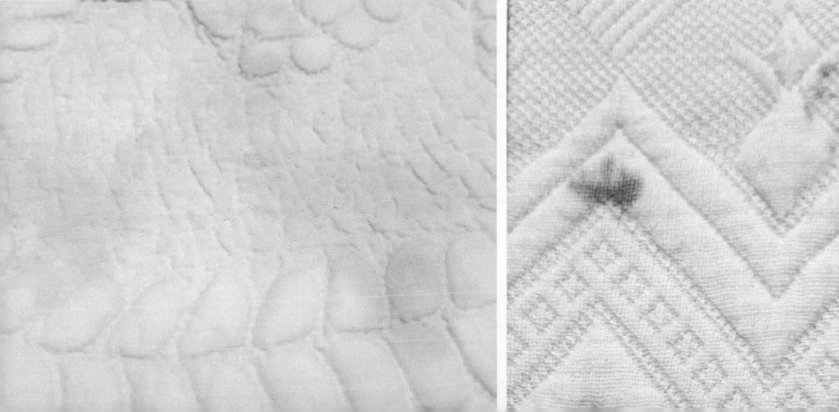

Wet-cleaning the textiles in a 0.2% surfactant solution, possibly with additional hydrogen peroxide solutions, helps reduce soil, stains, and discoloration. The wet-cleaning table (below left) allows textiles to lie flat, minimizing stress as they soak. Flax and cotton textiles are typically stronger wet than dry, but the age of the fibers negates this strength. The soaking also adds weight to the textiles, causing additional stress on the fabrics and stitches. Using a flat wet-cleaning table, these problems with washing are minimized.

After wet-cleaning, the table is raised to a slant that allows water to drain away. Conservators then use towels to remove excess water. The textile is moved to a drying table (below right), remaining flat on a carrying board. On the drying table, the textile is sandwiched between two cotton sheets, which are pressed down against the quilt for contact over the entire surface. As the textile dries, water moves to the cotton sheets and evaporates. This allows the textile to dry naturally, minimizing stress caused by faster drying methods.

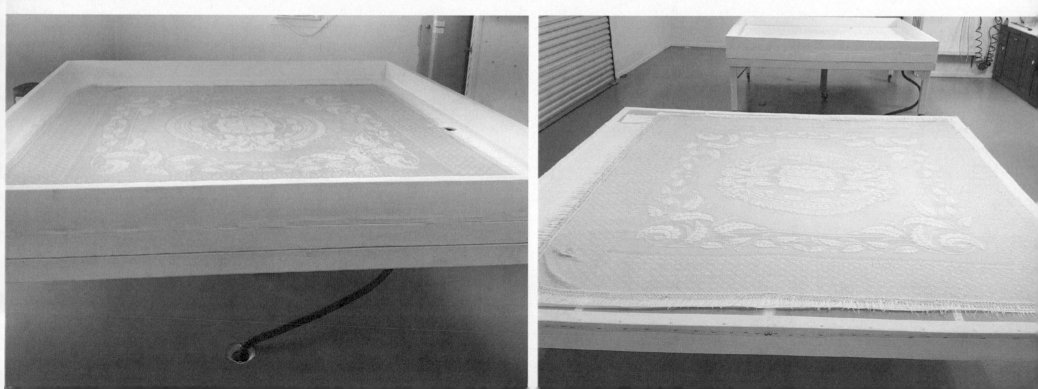

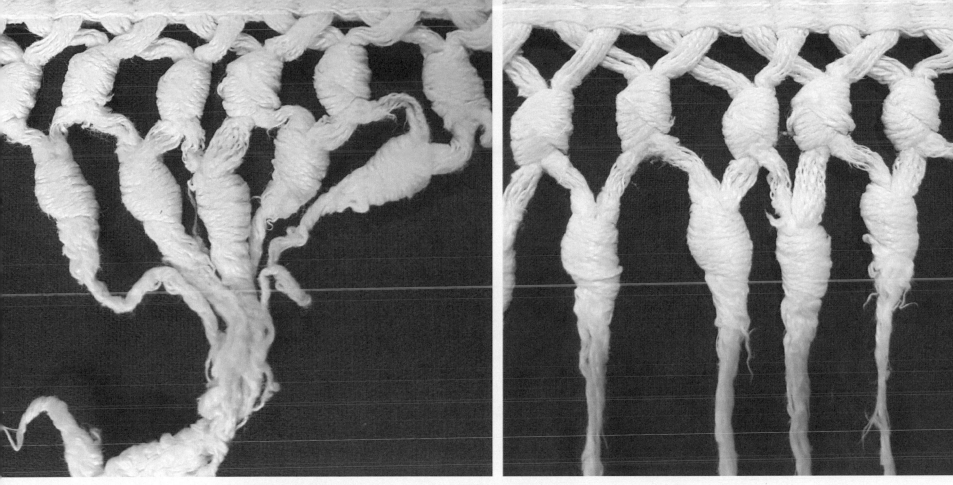

Marseilles quilt (Kentucky Museum, 1961.1.6) before (left) and after (right) treatment.

Fringes

Fringes can be a conservator's nightmare. For example, the Marseilles quilt (Kentucky Museum, 1961.1.6) had been laundered and heavily starched, leaving the fringe very entangled and stiff. Each tassel had to be freed individually.

Preparing for Exhibition

Once stabilized and cleaned, the textiles are ready to be prepared for display. Two-sided casings are applied to the part of the textile that will hang at the top, protecting the original textile from stress. Two rows of alternating running stitches attach the casing to the quilt, with the stitch penetrating through to the top of the quilt or counterpane. Stitches are long to incorporate enough yarns in the fabric to hold the stitch secure—the weaker the fabric, the longer the stitches. A line of machine stitches holds the two layers together with at least a half inch margin on each side. Then, a rod is inserted through the casings, which supports the textile while on display.

Melissa Smith of Camden, Tennessee, stitched the casings to the ten quilts and counterpanes.

Dr. Margaret Ordonez

Quilts and Counterpanes of Kentucky Women

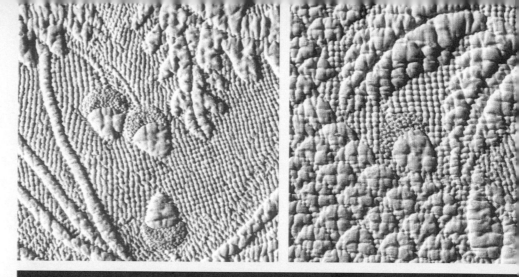

Rebecca Smith Washington (1781 - 1876) made this hand-quilted bedcover circa 1805. It is a rare surviving example of the influence of imported British woven "quilts." Her exquisitely stitched motifs mimic the framed-center format, intricate floral details, and filled background pattern of the popular manufactured textiles. The quilt reportedly "took seven years to stitch." Rebecca Smith was born in Virginia and married Whiting Washington, a nephew of George Washington. The couple moved to Russellville, Logan County, where they raised their family.

Wholecloth quilt, circa 1805. Kentucky Museum, 2652.

Unknown professional weaver, 1790 to 1820. Factories throughout England produced fancy bedcovers on specialized looms from American-grown cotton. The finished products, described as "quilted in the loom," were among the popular British textiles exported to the United States as fashionable consumer goods. In the years leading up to the War of 1812, patriotic women expressed support for an embargo against British textiles by creating their own embellished bedcovers.

Hand-woven "Marseilles quilt," 1790-1820. Kentucky Museum, 5157.

51

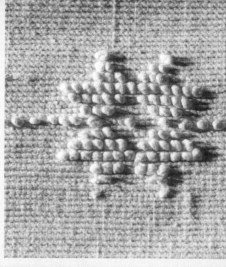

Anonymous British weaver, circa 1790 to 1820. This hand-woven counterpane was produced in Bolton, Lancashire, England, from American-grown cotton. One or two weavers worked a double-wide, two-harness loom to weave a bedcover without a center seam. This example would have been purchased as a fashionable consumer item, to be handed down as a family heirloom.

Bolton counterpane, 1790-1820. Kentucky Museum, 2857.

Anonymous professional weaver, circa 1800 to 1820. This counterpane is woven in the same weft-loop technique as those made in Bolton, Lancashire, England, but the format and the motifs are quite different. Some Bolton weavers continued to weave counterpanes after emigrating to the United States, where they modified motifs to suit American consumers.

Weft-loop woven counterpane, 1800-1820. Kentucky Historical Society, 2014.00.2.

Anne Lyne Starling (1777 - 1840) was born to a wealthy family in Mecklenburg County, Virginia. The flax and cotton in her counterpane were likely produced by enslaved farmhands, spinners, and weavers. In 1793, at age 16, she married Major John Holloway, age 31. By 1800, they were living on a 1,500-acre farm in Henderson County, Kentucky, where they raised cotton, flax, and other crops. By 1810, their household included eighteen enslaved laborers.

Embroidered counterpane, circa 1790. Kentucky Historical Society, 1980.12.1. (Images at left.)
and
Quilted table cover, circa 1790. Kentucky Historical Society, 1980.12.2. (Image on next page)

Maria Upshaw (1772 - 1852) was born in Essex, Virginia. As a young woman, Maria first embroidered an elegant white counterpane, then took the unusual step of turning it into a quilt, layering her embroidered panel onto batting and backing with close rows of tiny stitches. At age 29, Maria married Captain Nicholas Lafon, her first cousin. They lived in Frankfort before relocating to a farm in Woodford County, Kentucky. Maria's eldest daughter, Mary Virginia, embroidered a sampler, also in this exhibition. The quilt and sampler were passed down to Sallie Jackson.

Embroidered and quilted counterpane, circa 1790. Kentucky Historical Society, 1935.2.

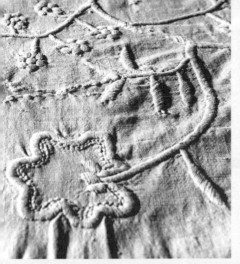

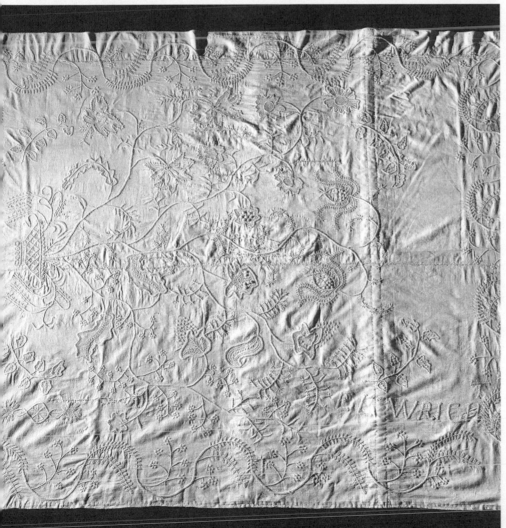

Miriam Elmina Helm (1777 - 1868) was born in Virginia in 1777 and came with her family to Kentucky. She created this elegant counterpane sometime before her marriage to Jacob Wright in 1797. By 1820, Miriam, Jacob, and their 13 children were living in Smiths Grove, Warren County. A granddaughter recalled, "Grandmother took great pains to teach her girls the art of spinning, weaving, and knitting. She did beautiful work herself. I have a counterpane for which she spun the thread, wove the cloth, and then embroidered, when a young girl. Grandmother wanted each of her girls to be a fine hand with a needle."

Embroidered counterpane, circa 1790. Kentucky Museum, 1987.86.1.

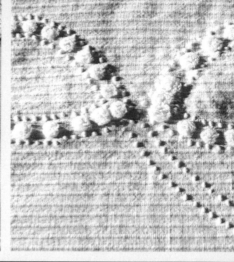

Rosannah Fisher (1781 - 1876) was born in Culpeper, Virginia. She embroidered her counterpane in a design of tufts on a handwoven ribbed fabric to reproduce the visual appearance of an imported Bolton counterpane. In 1806, at age 25, she married Martin Hardin. They raised their nine children on a farm in Mercer County, Kentucky. In 1860, Rosannah was widowed and her household included an enslaved family, identified in her late husband's will as "Jim, Judy, and their children."

Embroidered tufted counterpane, circa 1795. Kentucky Historical Society, 1981.16.

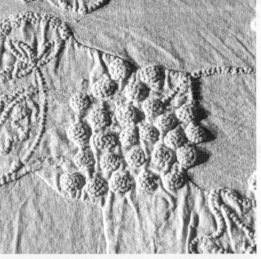
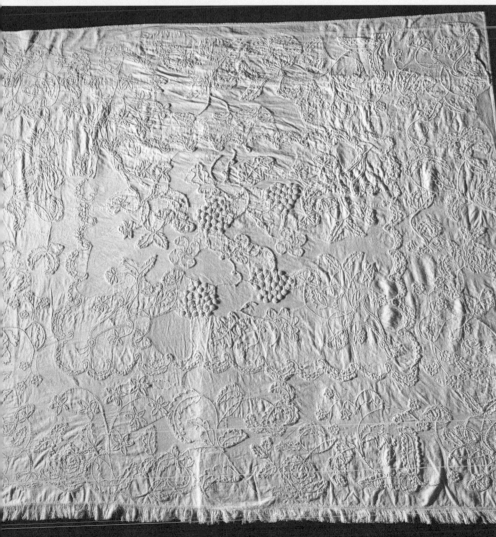

Charlotte Briggs (1795 - 1862) was born in Virginia, then moved to Warren County, Kentucky. She likely made this counterpane before her marriage to Thomas Stephens in 1817. By the time the counterpane came into the possession of Charlotte's granddaughter, Ora Susan Stephens Davenport (1866-1936), it had suffered from neglect, misuse, and damage. To preserve it, Ora Davenport washed the tattered remnants and carefully stitched them onto a new backing.

Tufted embroidered counterpane, circa 1805. Kentucky Museum, 1979.1.1.

Mary Walker Stith (1802 - 1884) was born in Bedford County, Virginia, before her family moved to Breckinridge County, Kentucky. According to family history, Mary "was taught needlework" at a Catholic school in Bethlehem, in Hardin County. She began work on this counterpane at age thirteen and finished it after her marriage. The fabric was made by an enslaved weaver named Morley.

Embroidered counterpane, 1813-1818. Metropolitan Museum of Art, 39.111.

For the exhibition, a reproduction photograph was displayed.

Anonymous enslaved weaver, circa 1823. This counterpane, handed down in one family, is a rare, surviving example of work by unnamed enslaved artisans. The family narrative states that "slaves made the thread from cotton and wove the coverlet" for Mary Leftwich Strange for her wedding in 1823.

Woven counterpane, circa 1823. Kentucky Historical Society, 1993.10.2.

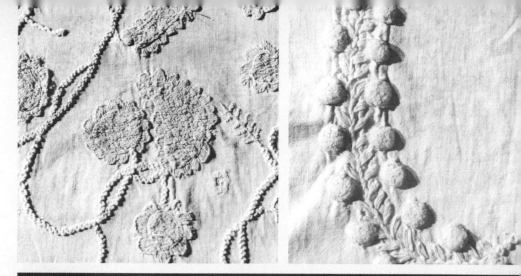

Sarah "Sallie" Darrough (1797 - 1874) was born in Harrison County, Kentucky. Her father, James Darrough, was born in Ireland, and her mother, Margaret Dobie, in Pennsylvania. Sallie married Jacob Hedger in 1818, at age 20, and they established a farm in Grant County, where they raised seven children. By 1870, the couple owned real estate and personal property valued at $26,000. Their household included a Black female household servant.

Embroidered counterpane, circa 1800. Kentucky Historical Society, 1937.7.

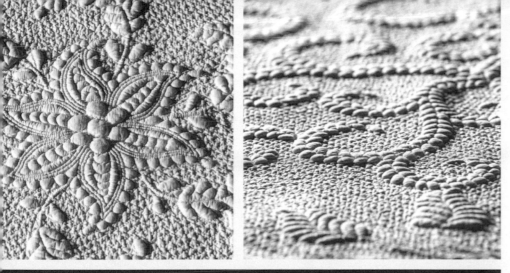

Temperance Wren Sharp (1783 - after 1850) made this white quilt before her 1816 marriage to John Sharp in Paint Lick, Garrard County, Kentucky. In 1851, her son, William, died at age 25. A month later, his young widow, Priscilla Brewer, gave birth to their daughter, Willia Sharp. Priscilla took the baby to her father's home in Mercer County, where grandmother Temperance and her daughter, also named Temperance, reportedly "used to spend months on visits" to the Brewer home.

Corded and stuffed quilt, circa 1800. Kentucky Museum, 1806.

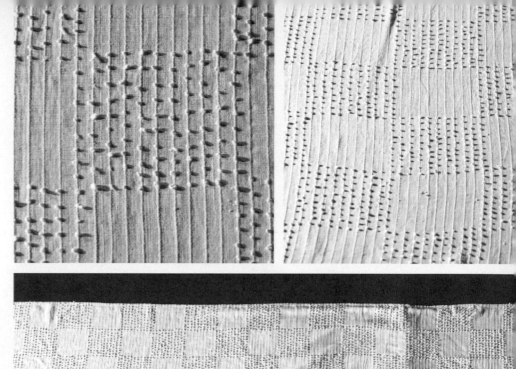

Elizabeth O'Neal (1786 - 1891) was born in Bloomfield, Nelson County, Kentucky, in 1786. Her mother, Fannie Hall, was a weaver whose parents had emigrated from West Yorkshire, England, to Fairfax, Virginia, around 1750. Elizabeth learned to weave from her mother. In 1804, she wove this white counterpane in a traditional weft-loop style that was practiced in Yorkshire and predated the more complex Bolton counterpanes woven in neighboring Lancashire.

Weft-loop woven counterpane, 1804. Kentucky Museum, KM2021.2.1.

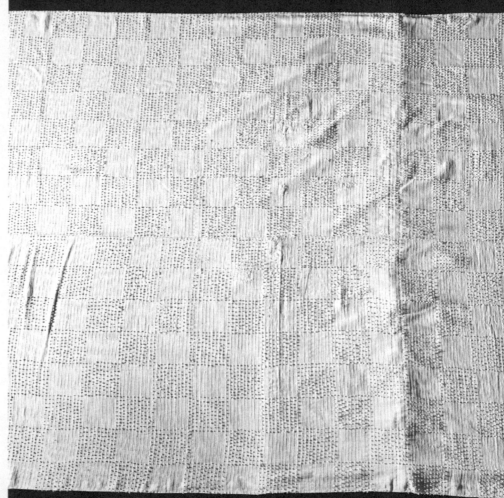

Martha "Patsy" Henry Woodruff (1786 - 1817) possibly recorded the date that she finished her counterpane. On June 10 of that year, she gave birth to a daughter, Emily Jane. On October 16, Martha died, and, according to custom, her name was given to her baby daughter: Martha Emily Jane Woodruff. The counterpane was handed down through the family. By the time the counterpane was donated by the maker's great-great-granddaughter, it was assumed that Martha Emily had made it and inscribed it with her birth date.

Embroidered tufted counterpane, dated 1817. Kentucky Historical Society, 2000.21.1.

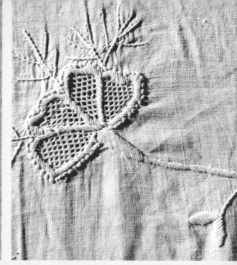

Elizabeth "Betsy" Patton Toomey was the granddaughter of Matthew Patton, who emigrated from Ireland, first to Virginia and then to Clark County, Kentucky. Her mother died soon after her birth, and "Betsy" was raised by her aunt, Elizabeth Yeager Patton. Betsy's counterpane includes Dresden work, which indicates that she learned embroidery at a female academy. The design of her counterpane closely resembles two others, pointing to a single unidentified instructor.

Embroidered counterpane, circa 1810.
Kentucky Historical Society, 1981.11.

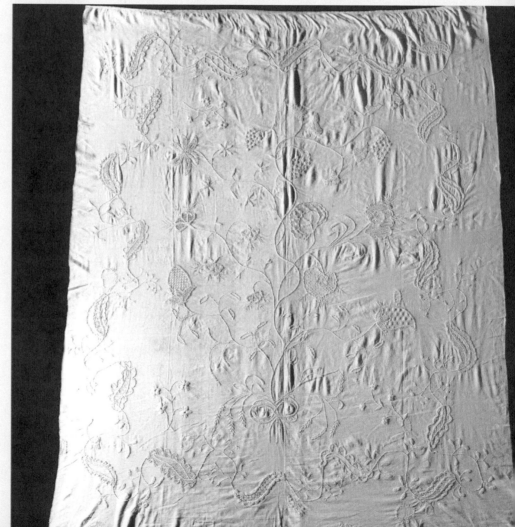

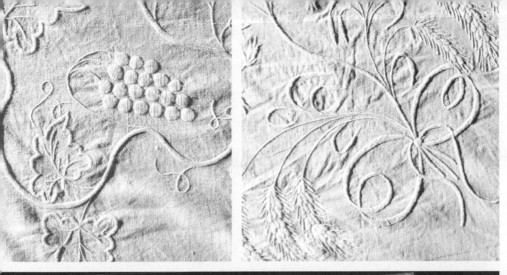

Anonymous needleworker, circa 1810. In 1981, the staff at the Kentucky Historical Society discovered this counterpane among a trove of uncatalogued early donations. The unknown maker learned to embroider from a skilled instructor, who probably drew the elegant design. Whoever she was, we know that the counterpane was treasured by her descendants, who preserved it in pristine condition.

Embroidered counterpane, circa 1810. Kentucky Historical Society, 1981.19.

Mary Virginia Lafon (1808 - 1880) embroidered this sampler at the age of 13. The text comes from a poem, "To a Young Lady," attributed to "Cotton," possibly a pseudonym for Cotton Mather (1663-1728), a New England clergyman and poet. Such verses were frequently published in early 19th century schoolbooks.

Schoolgirl sampler, dated 1821. Kentucky Historical Society, 1962.152.

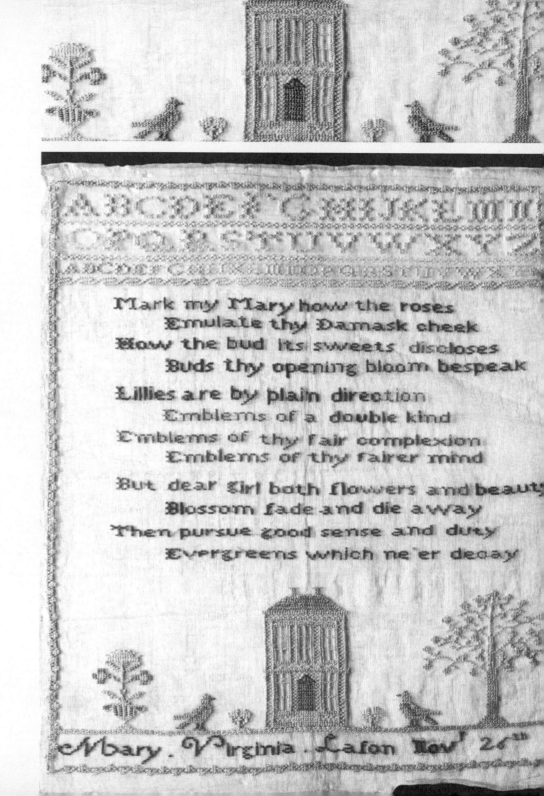

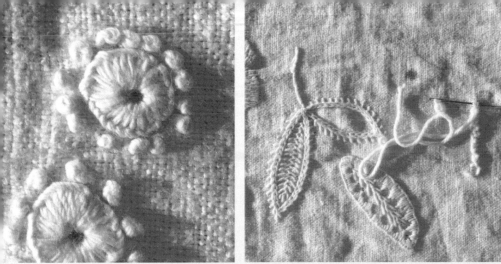

Anonymous needleworker, circa 1860 - 1900. In contrast with the formal samplers made by schoolgirls in female academies, this appears to be an informal practice sampler. The unknown maker started with a piece of linen toweling, stitching over designs marked in ink, probably drawn by a more experienced seamstress.

White "practice" sampler, 1860-1900. Kentucky Historical Society, 1976.1.46.

Anonymous needleworker, circa 1820. Tufted embroidered bedcovers first appeared in the late-18th century, inspired by woven counterpanes, such as examples elsewhere in this exhibition. Early examples typically mixed tufting with other stitches. This bedcover, from a later period, is covered with dense, high tufts in a bold, asymmetrical design of large, stylized flowers and leaves.

Tufted embroidered counterpane, circa 1820. Kentucky Historical Society, 1981.17.

70

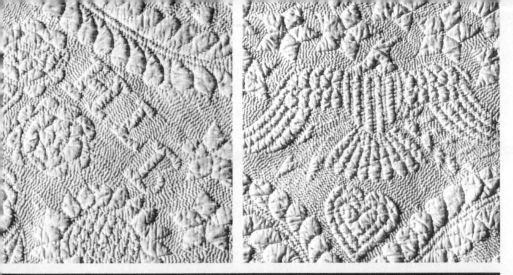

Harriet Legran Bates (1827 - after 1880) was born in Wayne County, Kentucky. By 1880, widowed and childless, she had returned to the family farm, headed by her widowed sister, Patience Jane Bates Simpson. The central medallion of Harriet's white quilt features cornucopias of pomegranates, grape bunches, and sheaves of grain. The Daughters of the American Revolution Museum owns two quilts with nearly identical center designs, both of which were made in Wayne County.

Quilt with center medallion, circa 1850. Kentucky Museum, 2002.11.1.

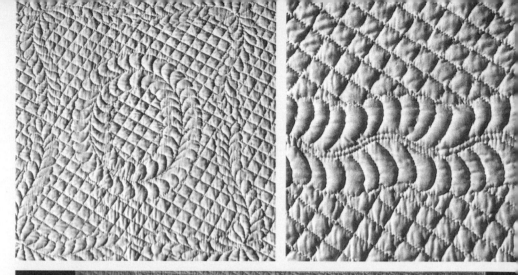

Gertrude Marie LaWarre Reuter (1898 - 1993) sewed and embroidered as a girl, but she did not discover quilting until she was in her 30s. Like many women, she made "packaged quilts," kits that included all of the materials needed to reproduce a professionally designed pattern. She also made quilts professionally in association with Sterns & Foster. The majority of her quilts were appliqué patterns, and this is the only white one among those in the Museum collection.

Medallion quilt, circa 1940. Kentucky Museum, 1999.44.7.

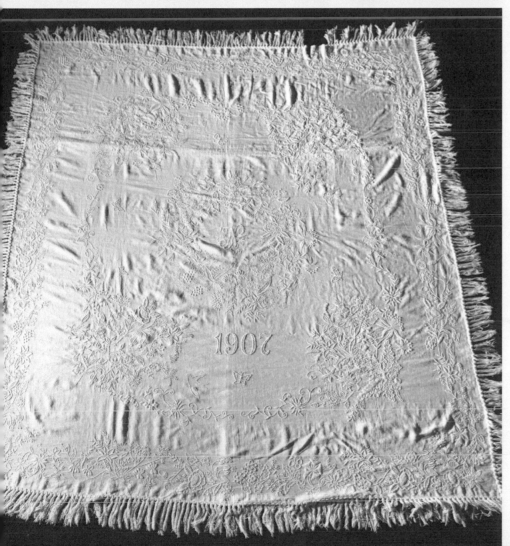

Betty Whitney Napier (1862 - 1916) was born in Allen County, Kentucky, the fourth of twelve children. She married Charles Napier, and they lived in Liberty, Casey County. In 1900, Bettie was widowed and living in Scottsville and described as a merchant, probably selling needlecraft supplies. Bettie executed the embroidery with great skill and artistry on a pre-stamped design on linen, adding an initial N and the year 1907.

Embroidered counterpane, dated 1907. Kentucky Museum, 1993.14.

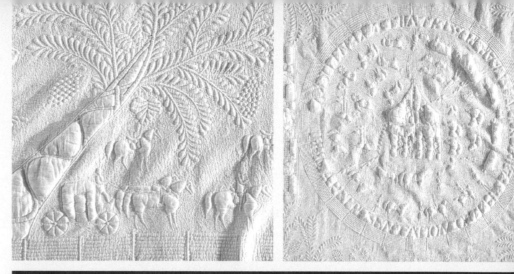

Virginia Mason Ivey (1828 - after 1880) was born in Tennessee and grew up in Keysburg, Logan County, Kentucky. As a young woman, she designed this whitework quilt to capture the excitement and lively interest of a county fairground. Virginia's needlework is often described as using needle and thread much like another artist might use pen or brush.

"A Representation of the Fair Ground near Russellville, Kentucky, 1856," stuffed and corded quilt, dated 1856. Division of Cultural and Community Life, National Museum of American History, Smithsonian Institution, TE.T10269.

For the exhibition, a reproduction photograph was displayed.

Credits

Guest Curator

Laurel Horton is an internationally acclaimed quilt researcher, author, editor, and lecturer who has studied and made quilts since 1975. Her numerous publications include books, research articles, book reviews, and popular articles. She consults with museums to curate exhibitions of historic quilts, write catalog essays, and prepare interpretive materials. Horton is a member of the American Quilt Study Group since 1982, and the former editor of *Uncoverings*, AQSG's annual volume of research papers. She has also, since 1990, taught quiltmaking at the John C. Campbell Folk School.

Contributors

Dr. Margaret Ordoñez is a former Professor of Textiles, Fashion Merchandising, and Design at the University of Rhode Island. She also served as Director of the Historic Textile Collection at the Textile and Conservation Laboratory and the Textile Gallery at the University of Rhode Island. She co-edited *Down By the Old Mill Stream: Quilts in Rhode Island* and, in 2004, was named a Fellow of the Costume Society. She currently serves as Professor Emerita at the University of Rhode Island.

Dr. Kate Brown is an Assistant Professor of History at Western Kentucky University, where she teaches courses focused on the American Founding Era, Early Republic, and American Legal History. She recently published *Alexander Hamilton and the Development of American Law* (University Press of Kansas, 2017), and was a 2003 Gilder Lehrman Fellow.

Sponsors

Kentucky
HISTORICAL SOCIETY

American Quilt Study Group

KENTUCKY
HUMANITIES

Quilter's Guild of Dallas

foundation
for advancement
in conservation

**Protecting Cultural
Heritage**

Donors of the Textiles

Kentucky Museum

Alice B. Colyard
Laurel McKay Horton
Josephine Johnson
Ora Colista Spradin Nicholls
Lula F. Pierce
Eliza Schwanderman
Wythe Washington

Kentucky Historical Society

Roseannah M. Burton
George Ann Carpenter
Janet Casey
Thomas L. Jones
Roger and Adsonia Martin
William Starling McCarroll
Mary M. McCormack
Laetitia I. Nutt
Elizabeth Riley
Louise Lisbet Roberts

Sources

Women

Boydston, Jeanne. *Home and Work: Housework, Wages, and the Ideology of Labor in the Early Republic*. New York: Oxford University Press, 1990.

Gunderson, Joan R. *To Be Useful to the World: Women in Revolutionary America, 1740-1790*. Chapel Hill: University of North Carolina Press, 2006.

Jabour, Anya. *Scarlett's Sisters: Young Women in the Old South*. Chapel Hill: University of North Carolina Press, 2007.

Kerber, Linda K. *Women of the Republic: Intellect and Ideology in Revolutionary America*.
Chapel Hill: University of North Carolina Press, 1980.

Miller, Marla R. *The Needle's Eye: Women and Work in the Age of Revolution*. Amherst: University of Massachusetts Press, 2006.

Norton, Mary Beth. *Liberty's Daughters: The Revolutionary Experience of American Women, 1750—1850*. Boston: Little, Brown and Company, 1980.

_____. "Reflections on Women in the Age of the American Revolution." in Hoffman, Ronald, and Peter J. Albert, eds. *Women in the Age of Revolution*. Charlottesville: University Press of Virginia, 1989. Pp. 479-493.

Stabile, Susan M. *Memory's Daughters: The Material Culture of Remembrance in Eighteenth- Century America*. Ithaca: Cornell University Press, 2004.

Zagarri, Rosemarie. *Revolutionary Backlash: Women and Politics in Early American Republic*. Philadelphia: University of Pennsylvania Press, 2007.

Cultural Context

Bushman, Richard L. *The Refinement of America: Persons, Houses, Cities*. New York: Alfred A. Knopf, 1992.

Heneghan, Bridget T. *Whitewashing America: Material Culture and Race in the Antebellum Imagination*. Jackson: University Press of Mississippi, 2003.

Horowitz, Morton J. *The Transformation of American Law: 1780-1860*. Cambridge: Harvard University Press, 1977.

Kleber, John E., ed. *The Kentucky Encyclopedia*. Lexington: University Press of Kentucky, 1992.

Tryon, Rolla M. *Household Manufactures in the United States, 1640-1860*. New York: Augustus Kelly, 1966.

Wood, Gordon S. *Empire of Liberty: A History of the Early Republic, 1789-1815*. New York: Oxford University Press, 2009.

Objects, files, family correspondence, documents, records, and archival materials: Kentucky Historical Society; Kentucky Museum, Western Kentucky University; Museum of Early Decorative Arts (MESDA); D.A.R. Museum; American Museum of History, Smithsonian; Antonio Ratti Textile Center, Metropolitan Museum; Winterthur Museum and Library; Colonial Williamsburg; Gateway Museum, Maysville KY; Loyal Jones Appalachian Center, Berea College; William Whitley House State Historic Site; Bolton Library and Museum, Bolton, Greater Manchester, UK; Ancestry.com.

Textile History

Beeston, Erin, and Laurel Horton. "Bolton's Cotton Counterpanes: Hand-Weaving in the Industrial Age." *Quilt Studies* 14, ed. Hazel Mills. Halifax: British Quilt Study Group, 2013, 7-36.

Berenson, Kathryn. *Marseille: The Cradle of White Corded Quilting*. Lincoln: University of Nebraska Press, 2010.

_____. "Quilted Works 'of Naples': The French and Italian Context of the Tristan Quilts," in *Quilt Studies* 13, ed. Hazel Mills. York: British Quilt Study Group, 2012.

Edwards, Michael M. *The Growth of the British Cotton Trade, 1780—1815*. New York: Augustus M. Kelly, 1967.

Pisani, Rosanna C. P., et al., eds. *The Guicciardini "Quilt": Conservation of the Deeds of Tristan*. Florence: Museo di Palazzo Davanzatti, 2010.

Wadsworth, Alfred P., and Julia De Lacy Mann. *The Cotton Trade and Industrial Lancashire, 1600—1780*. Manchester (U.K.): University of Manchester, 1931.

White Quilts and Counterpanes

Bakkom, Gail. "'Candlewicks': White Embroidered Counterpanes in America, 1790—1880," in *Uncoverings* 36, ed. Lynne Zacek Bassett (Lincoln NE: American Quilt Study Group, 2015), 61—92.

Horton, Laurel M. "Dresden Embroidery in Early Kentucky Counterpanes," in *The Social Fabric: Deep Local to Pan Global; Proceedings of the Textile Society of America 16th Biennial Symposium*. Presented at Vancouver, BC, Canada; September 19 – 23, 2018. https://digitalcommons.unl.edu/tsaconf/

_____. "Looking for Polly Armistead: Intimations of Mortality and Identity in an Embroidered Counterpane." *MESDA Journal* vol. 39 (2019). http://mesdajournal.org/.

_____. "Weft-loop Woven Counterpanes in the New Republic: The Rediscovery of a Textile Legacy." *Uncoverings* 2014, ed. Lynne Zacek Bassett. Lincoln NE: AQSG, 2014, 90- 114.

_____. "The Making of a Kentucky Counterpane," *Journal of Backcountry Studies* 8, no.1 Summer 2013). http://www.partnershipsjournal.org/.

CPSIA information can be obtained
at www.ICGtesting.com
Printed in the USA
LVRC091014030621
689239LV00002B/65